SHAMBHALA
25TH
ANNIVERSARY
1969-1994

A Touch of Grace

A TOUCH OF GRACE

Songs of Kabir

Translated by Linda Hess
and Shukdev Singh

SHAMBHALA
Boston & London
1994

Shambhala Publications, Inc.
Horticultural Hall
300 Massachusetts Avenue
Boston, Massachusetts 02115

9   8   7   6   5   4   3   2   1

First Shambhala Edition
Printed in the United States of America on acid-free paper ♾
Distributed in the United States by Random House, Inc.,
and in Canada by Random House of Canada Ltd

Library of Congress Cataloging-in-Publication Data

Kabir, 15th cent.
    A Touch of Grace: songs of Kabir/translated by Linda Hess and
Shukdev Singh.—1st Shambhala ed.
        p.   cm.—(Shambhala centaur editions)
    ISBN 0-87773-999-4
    I. Hess, Linda Beth.   II. Singh, Shukdev.   III. Title.
IV. Series.
    PK2095.K3A17   1994   94-9614
    891´.4312—dc20   CIP

Cover art: Painting of ritual design from Rajasthan (c. 1900),
copyright © Archaeological Survey of India.

Contents

Introduction

Heart says: When to move?
Mind says: When to leave?
For six months you rack your brain.
The town is half a mile away.

The voice of Kabir, coming from the North Indian town of Banaras, crossing several centuries in an old collection called the *Bijak*, gets into our ears and talks of the immediacy of solutions to what seem to be complex and knotted problems.

Im-mediacy: without mediation. Directly available.

Lost? So you were lost.
Wake up now.

Kabir says, seekers, listen:
Wherever you are
is the entry point.

Rainbird, to what far place
are you crying?
The world is overflowing
with that water.

The rainbird is a conventional figure in Indian religious poetry, representing intense de-
votion. It is in love with the special raindrops
that fall during a planetary conjunction, which
lasts for less than two weeks each year.
Through the rest of the year the rainbird

thirsts, unwilling to touch any water except the special drops that it loves and has dedicated its life to. It cries mournfully, longingly, during the interminable months of separation. (Some say its cry sounds like *"Piu kahan,"* which means, "Where is my beloved?") Kabir turns this convention around. Instead of relying on the evocative power of the separated lover's pain, he defuses the drama, disarms the device. There is no precious, inaccessible substance. The world is overflowing. Another couplet asks,

> When the river flows through your
>   own yard,
> how can you die of thirst?

Kabir's voice in the *Bijak* has a cutting edge. That character who flipflops and agonizes, searching her mind and heart, racking her brain for years over whether to take a step toward a goal that's fifteen minutes away, looks comical though she clearly takes herself very seriously. The momentous, self-dramatizing decisions, even (or especially) when they are about "spiritual" issues, are a coverup, an avoidance.

> The worldling ponders:
> domestic life or yoga?
> He loses his chances
> while others grow conscious.

Kabir observes the knots and complications.

> Hey swan, clear your mind
> in the morning. They've set
> so many snares, knit the net
> of three qualities

and trapped the world. . . .
Kabir says, if you meet the one
who can extricate you,
you won't forget it.

O Ram! The knot of confusion
won't loosen, so Death
keeps plucking you off.

Metaphors for the problem change. It can be
an ocean to drown in or a labyrinth to be lost
in:

Mind-ocean, mind-born waves—
don't let the tide
sweep you away.

The mind is a nervous thief,
the mind is a pure cheat.

The ruin of sages, men and gods,
the mind has a hundred thousand
gates.

Kabir insists that the solution is close at hand:

Kabir says, listen
to the word spoken
in every body.

If it's so simple, why does it seem so hard? Why don't all who hear Kabir's voice flock to follow his advice, drop their confusion, find the simple wisdom, drink the bountiful water?

The verses attributed to Kabir explore this question from many angles, exposing how our fears, attachments, habits, possessions, and fantasies keep us from opening our eyes to what we claim we want to see. The poet comes across as sharp, funny, and fearless. He undercuts authorities of all types, especially religious types who rely on their powers, techniques, and costumes to impress and take advantage. He has no patience with self-aggrandizing religionists, whether they be Brahmin priests, Muslim preachers, "posturing yogis," or greedy pilgrims.

Kabir has been characterized as a social reformer, satirist, mystic, and ecstatic—labels that all somewhat miss the mark. The bias of his work is to spark consciousness, one way or another, to wake people up, to liberate. He may do it by direct assault, trickery, dialogue, or dramatized example. His range is great. His understanding of human psychology is amazing. Liberation is basically a matter of achieving honesty—honesty in facing truth, whether it is the elaborate depths of our own greed or the fact of our any-minute-impending death, to name a couple of important examples.

Kabir lived, as far as anyone knows, in the fifteenth century in North India—some scholars say 1448–1518. His hometown was Banaras (also called Varanasi), on the banks of the holy Ganga River, then and now one of the most important Hindu pilgrimage centers. His socioeconomic status was low. The family belonged to a caste of weavers that had recently (perhaps in the preceding century or two) converted to Islam. Muslims, while remaining a minority in largely Hindu India, had ruled much of the subcontinent since about 1200 and would do so until the ascendancy of the British in the mid-eighteenth century. The ensuing cultural and political adjustments included many conversions. A fairly common occurrence was for low artisan castes to convert en masse, lured by the more egalitarian social ideology of Islam, by the wish to link their fate to the ruling powers, and by the attractive teachings of Sufi masters, who had much in common with the gurus and poet-saints of popular Hindu devotionalism (bhakti). The Sufis, or Muslim mystics, were organized into orders, which made teaching more systematic and efficient. They (like the bhakti teachers) tended to be down-to-earth, lacking pretension and ostentation, while at the same time passionate and charismatic, fired by music and poetry of personal experience, commitment, and love.

Kabir's name is Muslim, but his imagery and ways of approaching truth show more influence of Hindu and Buddhist traditions than of Islam. Legend makes him the disciple of a famous Hindu guru, Ramananda: a popular story shows how the weaver tricked the Brahmin into accepting him as a student. In Kabir's poetry, Ram is the preferred name for God, though it seems clear that he does not mean the anthropomorphic avatar of the devotional *Ramayana* narratives. Ram is offered as an all-powerful name, a mantra, a sign of the supreme being who is beyond description.

Kabir is preeminent among poets associated with the *nirgun* tendency in North Indian bhakti—that is, the tendency to worship a

God who has no form, no physical images, no incarnations or narratives. Though this seems to go against the grain of popular Hinduism, in which images, narratives, and avatars are so important, Kabir has been easily enfolded into the circle of revered saints and poetic geniuses, side by side with the *sagun* poets (worshipers of God-in-form) and with those who float back and forth between *nirgun* and *sagun* perspectives.

All the stories about Kabir are legends, based on little or no historical evidence. The number and variations of stories have increased over time. All agree that he was a Muslim weaver. Most traditions say he was illiterate. His compositions would certainly have been presented to the world in oral form, sung or chanted, then transmitted orally, and altered as they moved through the countryside.

How and when did the songs get written down? The most important collections that we have were inscribed by members of *nirgun* sects and kept in those sects' manuscript collections. In the sixteenth century, the Sikh Panth (sect) was taking shape in Punjab, the Dadu Panth in Rajasthan, and the Kabir Panth in parts of present Uttar Pradesh and Bihar. The Sikh holy book, codified in its final form around 1604, contains many verses attributed to Kabir. More are found in the Dadu Panthi anthologies and in the "eastern tradition" of the Kabir Panth. The *Bijak* belongs to this eastern tradition. It was probably compiled in the seventeenth century, at least a hundred years after the poet's death; some parts of present-day printed versions are likely to have been added later.

We will never know exactly what came out of Kabir's mouth. He would have had sharp words for academicians who make hairsplitting efforts to authenticate this line or eradicate that one, meanwhile ignoring what the lines say. We can see the main contours of his message, the uniqueness of his style, the themes and images that come up repeatedly, the great variety of what he (or those inspired by him) observed and commented on, and the ways in which collections change from one region or time period to another. Scholarly studies of the texts and their histories are available for those who want to know more.

"Liberation" in the context of Indian religious traditions—called by names like *mukti* or *moksha*, *nirvana* or *sahaja samadhi*—has generally meant getting out of the cycle of birth and death, the turning worlds of suffering and delusion, known as *samsara*. This kind of liberation seems to emphasize separation from life. In one important philosophical school, the word for liberation is *kaivalya*, or isolation. But there are also certain strands in Hindu and Buddhist traditions in which spiritual liberation can and should occur amidst continuing rebirths. Bhakti Hinduism and Mahayana Buddhism emphasize connection—love of God for the former, interdependence of all beings for the latter. In these contexts, one gets liberated not from life, death, and the world, but from limited self-concepts and grasping habits.

In the twentieth century, *liberation* often has political meanings. Because Kabir was iconoclastic and anti-institutional, because he was aggressive in challenging elites, and because he was poor and low in status, some would like to call him a revolutionary, implying that he was actively political, a model for liberationists of our time. This characterization doesn't ring true. Modern notions of grassroots activism against oppressive systems don't fit the fifteenth-century picture. Kabir shared the sexist attitudes of his time: women rarely make an appearance in the *Bijak* except to represent sex, temptation, and delusion. He doesn't seem to favor any group over any other: His barbs strike rag-clad yogis, sleazy pandits, landlords, tenants, and customers in the vegetable market. He never shows concern about poverty or governing powers.

His prime interest, we must grant, is in a *spiritual* liberation, a transforming of consciousness. But the process of transformation is often quite down-to-earth. It involves facing up to every bit of self-delusion and dishonesty, facing up to the fear of all deaths, large and small. It involves using language in ways that range from the most plain and direct to the most oblique and riddling.

One Kabir legend tells how, when he died, the Hindus lined up on one side, the Muslims on the other, to fight over the right to dispose of his body. Though both camps had been offended by him when he was alive, both wanted to identify with his sanctity after he died. They had doctrinal differences about the funeral ritual. Muslims prefer to bury their dead, Hindus to cremate. Muslims intone verses from the Koran, while Hindus favor Vedic mantras. Kabir's body, covered with a cloth, was laid out between the quarreling parties. Swords were drawn. Just when bloodshed seemed inevitable, someone pulled the cloth away to discover not a body but a pile of flowers. The two sides divided the flowers, and each burned or buried its half.

In this story, even Kabir's corpse laughs at the idiocy of sectarian zealots who, in fighting over his remains, show that they never understood a word he said. It's no surprise that similar dramas continue to the present time. In late 1992, mobs of excited Hindus in a North Indian city demolished a mosque that was probably built about a decade after Kabir's death. They were liberating the spot, they said, for a grand temple to their god Ram, believed to have been born right there. Kabir's five-hundred-year-old observation sounds fresh:

The Hindu says Ram is the Beloved,
the Turk says Rahim.
Then they kill each other.
Nobody knows the secret.

Kabir may not have been a political activist,
but his words are useful to people presently
concerned with healing injustice and violence.
In the struggle over the mosque-and-temple
site, those who wish to promote communal
harmony and to disarm the polarizing forces
of religious nationalism often quote Kabir.

Were his interests spiritual? If so, the spiritual for him stretched far, like the cloth of the
weaver who "spread his warp through the universe." Those interests included anger at killers
of animals, criticism of careless and cruel talk,
mockery of circumcision and sacred threads,

withering dismissal of caste distinctions, and wondering observation of self-deceiving selfishness:

> As the city blazes, the watchman
> sleeps happily, thinking,
> "My house is secure.
> Let the town burn, as long as my
>   things are saved."
> Ram, how your colors flicker!

And, let's not forget, Kabir's interests included an experience of God, truth, or reality.

> Dance done without feet,
> tune played without hands,
> praises sung without tongue,
> singer without shape or form,
> the true teacher reveals.

Of the sourceless state, what to say?
No town, nowhere to stay;
seen without a trace;
what do you call that place?

Wherever I look,
only this, only this.
The diamond pierced
my ruby heart.

Kabir says,
I've said and I've said.
I'm tired of saying.

Linda Hess
Berkeley, California
June 1994

A Touch of Grace

Saints, I see the world is mad.
If I tell the truth they rush to beat me,
if I lie they trust me.
I've seen the pious Hindus, rule-followers,
early morning bath-takers—
killing souls, they worship rocks.
They know nothing.
I've seen plenty of Muslim teachers, holy men
reading their holy books
and teaching their pupils techniques.
They know just as much.
And posturing yogis, hypocrites,
hearts crammed with pride,
praying to brass, to stones, reeling
with pride in their pilgrimage,
fixing their caps and their prayer-beads,
painting their brow-marks and arm-marks,
braying their hymns and their couplets,

reeling. They never heard of soul.
The Hindu says Ram is the Beloved,
the Turk says Rahim.
Then they kill each other.
No one knows the secret.
They buzz their mantras from house to house,
puffed with pride.
The pupils drown along with their gurus.
In the end they're sorry.
Kabir says, listen saints:
they're all deluded!
Whatever I say, nobody gets it.
It's too simple.

Saints, if I speak
who will believe it?
If I lie
it passes for truth.
I glimpsed a jewel,
unpierced and priceless,
without buyer or seller.
Glittering, gleaming, it flashed
in my eyes, and filled
the ten directions.
A touch of grace
from the guru:
the invisible, markless
appeared.
Simple meditation,
absolute stillness
awakened. Simply
I met Ram.

Wherever I look,
only this, only this.
The diamond pierced
my ruby heart.
Through the guru
comes the supreme.
Thus teaches Kabir.

Saints, I've seen both ways.
Hindus and Muslims don't want discipline,
they want tasty food.
The Hindu keeps the eleventh-day fast
eating chestnuts and milk.
He curbs his grain but not his brain
and breaks his fast with meat.
The Turk prays daily, fasts once a year,
and crows "God! God!" like a cock.
What heaven is reserved for people
who kill chickens in the dark?
For kindness and compassion
they've cast out all desire.
One kills with a chop, one lets the blood drop,
in both houses burns the same fire.
Turks and Hindus have one way,

the guru's made it clear.
Don't say Ram, don't say Khuda.
So says Kabir.

Saints, the Brahmin is a slicked-down butcher.
He slaughters a goat and rushes for a buffalo
without a twinge of pain in his heart.
He lounges after his bath, slaps sandalpaste
on his brow, does a song and dance
for the Goddess, crushes souls
in the wink of an eye—
the river of blood flows on.
How holy! What a superior race! What
    authority
in society, and how people grovel
to get his initiation!
It makes me laugh.
They tell tales about ending sin
but their actions are base.
I've seen two of them throttle each other,

but Yama carted off both.
Kabir says, saints, this is Kaliyug:
the age of phony Brahmins.

Without Hari he's befuddled,
without a guru he's a mess.
Everywhere he goes
he loses himself
in nets within nets.
The yogi says, "Yoga's the top,
don't talk of seconds."
Tuft of hair, shaven head, matted locks, vow
    of silence—
who's gotten anywhere?
Brainy ones, gifted ones,
heroes, poets, benefactors
cry, "I'm the greatest!"
They all go back where they came from
and don't take anything along.
Drop that wretched right hand and left

and grab Hari's feet—these very feet!
Kabir says, the dumb man has tasted sugar.
If you ask, what will he say?

O Ram! The knot of confusion
won't loosen, so Death
keeps plucking you off.
Monks and yogis give up their pedigrees
but still brag of their lineage.
Knowers and heroes, poets, philanthropists,
people with all sorts of talents
can't break through
this state of mind.
They read hymns, legends and laws
but miss the experience.
How can iron turn to gold
without touching the touchstone?
If you don't cross over alive,
how can you cross when you're dead?
Alive, you're not crossing!
Wherever you put your faith,
that's where you'll be at death.

Clever man! Whatever you've done,
wise or foolish, try to understand.
Kabir asks: what can you say about people
who don't see what they're staring at?

Brother, where did your two gods come from?
Tell me, who made you mad?
Ram, Allah, Keshav, Karim, Hari, Hazrat—
so many names.
So many ornaments, all one gold,
it has no double nature.
For conversation we make two—
this *namāz*, that *pujā*,
this Mahadev, that Muhammed,
this Brahma, that Adam,
this a Hindu, that a Turk,
but all belong to earth.
Vedas, Korans, all those books,
those Mullas and those Brahmins—
so many names, so many names,
but the pots are all one clay.
Kabir says, nobody can find Ram,

both sides are lost in schisms.
One slaughters goats, one slaughters cows,
they squander their birth in isms.

Dear swan, where will you go
when you leave the lake?
You used to peck up pearls there
and taste such pleasures—
now water shrinks from the leaves,
the bed is dry, the lotus withers.
What's taken away today, says Kabir,
will it come again tomorrow?

That con man Hari has conned the world,
but brother, who can live without him?
Who's whose husband? Who's whose wife?
Death's gaze spreads—untellable story.
Who's whose father? Who's whose son?
Who suffers? Who dies?
With his conjuring he snatches away
your roots. No one can see
Ram's trickery.
Kabir's heart accepts the thief.
Cheating disappears
when you recognize the cheat.

The blessed one wanders free as a swan
speaking the spotless name.
With a pearl in his beak he lures the world,
silent or singing God's fame.
On Mansarovar's shore he dwells,
cool at the feet of Ram.
No stupid crow can come near
that visionary swan.
Those who can separate milk from water,
I call them mine, says Kabir.

The trickster Hari roves through the world
pulling tricks, and saying
nothing. Oh childhood friend,
when you left me,
where did you go that morning?
You're the only man,
I'm your woman.
Your footstep is heavier than stone.
The flesh is clay, the body air.
I'm afraid of Hari's tricks,
says Kabir.

Hermit, that yogi is my guru
who can untie this song.
A tree stands without root,
without flowers bears fruit;
no leaf, no branch, and eight
sky-mouths thundering.
Dance done without feet,
tune played without hands,
praises sung without tongue,
singer without shape or form—
the true teacher reveals.
Seek the bird's, the fish's path.
Kabir says, both are hard.
I offer myself to an image:
the great being beyond boundaries
and beyond beyond.

Pandit, do some research
and let me know
how to destroy transiency.
Money, religion, pleasure, salvation—
which way do they stay, brother?
North, South, East, or West?
In heaven or the underworld?
If God is everywhere, where is hell?

Heaven and hell are for the ignorant,
not for those who know Hari.
The fearful thing that everyone fears,
I don't fear.
I'm not confused about sin and purity,
heaven and hell.
Kabir says, seekers, listen:
Wherever you are
is the entry point.

Pandit, look in your heart for knowledge.
Tell me where untouchability
came from, since you believe in it.
Mix red juice, white juice and air—
a body bakes in a body.
As soon as the eight lotuses
are ready, it comes
into the world. Then what's
untouchable?
Eighty-four hundred thousand vessels
decay into dust, while the potter
keeps slapping clay
on the wheel, and with a touch
cuts each one off.
We eat by touching, we wash
by touching, from a touch
the world was born.

So who's untouched? asks Kabir.
Only he
who has no taint of Maya.

Pandit, you've got it wrong.
There's no creator or creation there,
no gross or fine, no wind or fire,
no sun, moon, earth or water,
no radiant form, no time there,
no word, no flesh, no faith,
no cause and effect, nor any thought
of the Veda. No Hari or Brahma,
no Shiva or Shakti, no pilgrimage
and no rituals. No mother, father
or guru there. Is it two or one?
Kabir says, if you understand now,
you're guru, I'm disciple.

Think, pandit, figure it out:
male or female?
In a Brahmin's house she's Mrs. Brahmin,
in a yogi's she's a disciple.
Reading the Koran she's a Turkish lady.
In Kaliyug she lives alone.
She doesn't choose a husband,
doesn't get married,
but has sons.
Not a single black-haired fellow escapes her,
but she's a permanent virgin.
She stays with her mother,
doesn't join her in-laws,
won't sleep with her husband.
Kabir says, he lives from age to age
who drops his family, caste and race.

Pandit, think
before you drink
that water.
That house of clay you're sitting in—
all creation is pouring through it.
Fifty-five million Yadavs soaked there,
and eighty-eight thousand sages.
At every step a prophet is buried.
All their clay has rotted.
Fish, turtles and crocodiles
hatched there. The water is thick
with blood. Hell flows
along that river, with
rotten men and beasts.
Trickling through bones, melting through
        flesh—
where does milk come from?
That's what you drink after lunch, pandit.

And you call clay untouchable?
Throw out your holy scriptures, pandit,
those fantasies of your mind.
Kabir says, listen, Brahmin:
All this
is your own doing.

Think about it, knower of Brahma.
It's pouring, pouring, the thunder's roaring,
but not one raindrop falls.
An elephant's tied to an ant's foot,
a sheep eats a wolf,
a fish jumps out of the ocean
and builds a house on the beach.
Frog and snake lie down together,
a cat gives birth to a dog,
the lion quakes in fear of the jackal—
these marvels can't be told.
Who tracks down the deer of doubt
in the forest? The archer aims,
trees burn in the sea,
a fish plays hunter.
Oh, what marvelous knowledge!

If anyone can hear,
he'll fly to the sky without wings
and live, not die, says Kabir.

Hey pandits, who didn't die?
If you find out, tell me.
Brahma, Vishnu and Shiva died,
Parvati's son Ganesha died,
so many suns and moons died,
Hanuman the bridgebuilder died,
Krishna died, the maker died.
One, the Original, didn't die.
No fall, no rise.
Kabir says, that one never dies.

If you can see that tree
you'll be free
from age and death.
The tree is a whole world.
From one trunk burst three boughs,
the middle bough has four fruits,
and leaves and branches—who can count
    them?
A creeper clings to the three
spheres, wraps tight
so even the wise ones
can't get free.
Kabir says, I go on shouting
and the pandits go on thinking.

Brother, come see what people call
    security.
This tale is untellable.
Lion and tiger are yoked to a plow
sowing rice in a barren field.
The wild bear is pulling weeds,
the billy goat runs the farm.
The nanny goat married a lion
while a cow sang wedding songs.
The dowry was an antelope,
the bridesmaid was a lizard.
The crow washed all the laundry
while the heron gnashed its teeth.
The fly shaved its head, shouting,
I must join the marriage party!
Kabir says, can you
figure out this
poetry?

If so I'll call you
scholar, genius,
devotee.

Lord!
A fire is raging
without fuel.
No one can put it out.
I know it spreads from you, enflaming
the whole world.
Even in water
the flames sprout.
Not one but nine streams
are burning. No one
knows any device.
As the city blazes, the watchman
sleeps happily, thinking,
"My house is secure.
Let the town burn, as long as my things
are saved."
Ram, how your colors flicker!
In a hunchback's arms can a man's desires

be fulfilled?
Even as you think of this, you disappear
from birth to birth, your body forever
unsatisfied. No one is so stupid
as one who knows this
and pretends he doesn't.
Kabir asks, what's the way out
for such a fool?

Maya's the super swindler.
Trailing the noose of three qualities,
she wanders, whispering
honeyed words.
For Vishnu she's Lakshmi,
For Shiva she's Shakti,
for priests an idol,
for pilgrims a river.
To a monk she's a nun,
to a king she's a queen,
in one house a jewel,
in one a shell.
For devotees she's a pious lady,
for Brahma, Mrs. Brahma.
Kabir says, seekers,
listen well:
this is a story
no one can tell.

When you die, what do you do with your
    body?
Once the breath stops
you have to put it away.
There are several ways to deal
with spoiled flesh.
Some burn it, some bury it
in the ground.
Hindus prefer cremation,
Turks burial.
But in the end, one way or another,
both have to leave home.
Death spreads the karmic net
like a fisherman snaring fish.
What is a man without Ram?
A dung beetle in the road.

Kabir says, you'll be sorry later
when you go from this house
to that one.

The yogi's gone away again
to a town of five women
in another country,
no one knows where.
He won't come back to his cave.
His rags are burnt, his flag torn,
his stick snapped, his bowl cracked.
Kabir says, This miserable Kaliyug!
What's in the pot
comes out the spout.

If seed is form is god,
then, pandit,
what can you ask?
Where is the intellect? ego? heart?
the three qualities?
Nectar and poison bloom,
fruits ripen,
the Vedas show many ways
to cross the sea.
Kabir says, what do I know
of you or me,
of who gets caught
and who goes free?

The musician plays a peerless instrument
with eight sky-mouths thundering.
Only you are played, only you
thunder, your hand alone
runs up and down.
In one sound thirty-six ragas, speaking
an endless word.
The mouths a shaft,
the ear a sounding gourd—
the true teacher made the instrument.
The tongue a string,
the nose a peg—
he rubs on the wax of Maya.
Light bursts in the sky-temple
at a sudden
reversal.

Kabir says, clarity comes
when the musician lives
in your heart.

Beast-meat and man-meat are the same, both
    have blood that's red, sir.
Men eat beasts, but even jackals shun a man
    that's dead, sir.
The potter Brahma shaped the earth; death,
    birth—where do things pass, sir?
But you eat animals and fish as if they grew
    like grass, sir.
For gods and goddesses of clay you slaughter
    a living beast, sir.
If your god's real, why can't he go to the field
    and have his feast, sir?
Kabir says, saints, say Ram, Ram, and Ram
    and Ram again, sir.
The things men eat to please their tongues
    come back to eat the men, sir.

Rainbird, to what far place
are you crying?
The world is overflowing
with that water.
The water where sound and sea
divide, where Vedas
and six rites are born,
where dwell
both god and soul,
that water holds earth,
sky and light.
The water from which all bodies spring—
who knows its secret?
Not even Kabir.

You go around
bent! bent! bent!
Your ten doors are full of hell, you smell
like a fleet of scents,
your cracked eyes don't see the heart,
you haven't an ounce of sense.
Drunk with anger, hunger, sex,
you drown without water.
If you're burnt, the ashes mix with dust;
if you're buried, the maggots eat.
Otherwise you're food for pigs, dogs, crows.
Thus I praise the flesh.
Enchanted madman! You don't see or think—
death isn't far from you.
Try a thousand ways, but still the body
ends up dust.
The fool doesn't have a thought
as he sits in his house of sand.

But without the one Ram, says Kabir,
the cleverest too
are swamped.

It's a heavy confusion.
Veda, Koran, holiness, hell, woman, man,
a clay pot shot with air and sperm . . .
When the pot falls apart, what do you call it?
Numskull! You've missed the point.
It's all one skin and bone, one piss and shit,
one blood, one meat.
From one drop, a universe.
Who's Brahmin? Who's Shudra?
Brahma *rajas*, Shiva *tamas*, Vishnu *sattva* . . .
Kabir says, plunge into Ram!
There: No Hindu. No Turk.

The self forgets itself
as a frantic dog in a glass temple
barks himself to death;
as a lion, seeing a form in the well,
leaps on the image;
as a rutting elephant sticks his tusk
in a crystal boulder.
The monkey has his fistful of sweets
and won't let go. So
from house to house
he gibbers.
Kabir says, parrot-on-a-pole:
who has caught you?

Many hoped
but no one found
Hari's heart.
Where do the senses rest?
Where do the Ram-chanters go?
Where do the bright ones go?
Corpses: all gone
to the same place.
Drunk on the juice
of Ram's bliss,
Kabir says,
I've said and I've said.
I'm tired of saying.

Make your own decision.
See for yourself while you live.
Find your own place.
Dead, what house will you have?
Creature, you don't see
your opportunity.
In the end no one belongs to you.
Kabir says, it's difficult,
this wheel of time.

They're morons and mindless fools
who don't know Ram in every breath.
You rampage in, knock down a cow,
cut her throat and take her life.
You turn a living soul to a corpse
and call it a holy rite.
You say the meat is pure, brother?
How was it born? Listen:
Meat is made of blood and sperm,
that's your unholy dinner.
Fool! You say, "It's not our sin,
but our forefathers' preaching."
The blood they shed is on your head
who taught you such a teaching.
The hair is white that once was black
but the heart's as black as before.
Why chant and shout, why pray
till you drop dead at the mosque door?

Pandits read Puranas, Vedas,
Mullas learn Muhammed's faith.
Kabir says, both go straight to hell
if they don't know Ram in every breath.

It's not a wild beast, brother,
not a wild beast,
but everyone eats
the meat.
The beast is a whole world—
unimaginable!
Tear open the belly,
no liver or guts.
It's this kind of meat, brother:
every minute sold.
Bones and hooves on the dump—
fire and smoke
won't eat it.
No head, no horn,
and where's a tail?
All the pandits meet
and fight.
Kabir sings a marriage song.

Lucky one! Why waste this precious life
   through greed?
In the field of former lives you sowed the seed.
From a drop to a shape, you stayed in the pool
   of fire;
Ten months in your mother, then again seized
   by desire.
Again youth, again old age, what had to pass
   has passed.
Yama ties you and takes you away. The tears
   flow fast.
Don't hope for life, time owns your
   breath—Kabir's advice:
It's a gambler's world. Before you throw the
   dice, think twice.

What will you call the pure?
Say, creature: how will you mutter the
    name
of one without hand or foot,
mouth, tongue or ear?
The light called light-within-light,
what is its sign?
When light-within-light is killed by
    light,
where has it gone?
They say Brahma
made the Veda,
but he couldn't get
this state.
Kabir says, seekers, sages, scholars,
listen and penetrate.

Who will be sheriff
in a town littered with meat
where the watchman
is a vulture?
Mouse in the boat,
cat at the oars;
frog sleeping,
snake on guard;
bull giving birth,
cow sterile,
calf milked
morning, noon and night;
lion forever leaping
to fight the jackal.
Kabir says, rare listeners
hear the song right.

Where are you going alone, my friend?
You don't get up, or fuss
about your house.
The body fed on sweets, milk and butter,
the form you adorned
has been tossed out.
The head where you carefully
tied the turban,
that jewel,
the crows are tearing open.
Your stiff bones burn
like a pile of wood,
your hair like a bunch of grass.
No friend comes along, and where
are the elephants you had tied?
You can't taste Maya's juice,
a cat called death has pounced inside.
Even now you lounge in bed

as Yama's club
falls on your
head.

I looked and looked—astonishing!
(Only a rare one hears me sing.)
The earth shot backwards to the sky,
an elephant fell in an ant's eye,
mountains flew without a breeze,
souls and creatures climbed the trees,
in a dry lake the waves lashed,
without water, waterbirds splashed.
Pandits sat and read the law,
babbled of what they never saw.
Who understands Kabir's rhyme
is a true saint to the end of time.

Son of a slut!
There. I've insulted you.
Think about getting on the good road.
You don't even dream of meeting
the master of your house.
Brahmin, Kshatriya, Bania
don't listen to what I say.
Yogis and creeping creatures
follow their own way;
and yogis at their leisure
don't withdraw
from pleasure.

You simple-minded people!
As water enters water, so Kabir
will meet with dust.
"That Maithili pandit said
you'd die near Magahar.
What a terrible place to be dead!
If you want Ram to take you away,
die somewhere else instead.
Besides, they say
whoever dies at Magahar
comes back a donkey."

So much for your faith in Ram.
What's Kashi? Magahar? Barren ground,
when Ram rules in your heart.
If you give up the ghost in Kashi
is there some debt
on the Lord's part?

How will you cross, Yogi,
how will you cross,
so full of crookedness?
Look how he meditates,
serves and prays.
Look: the white plumage,
the crane's sly ways.
Mood of a snake, look:
utterly lewd,
utterly quarrelsome,
utterly shrewd.
Look: a hawk's
face, and the thoughts
of a cat.
Schools of philosophy
like a cloak furled.
Look: the witch vanity
gulps down the world.

The bee has flown, the heron remains.
Night is over,
day is going too.
The young girl quakes and shivers,
not knowing what her lover
will do.
Water won't stay
in unbaked clay.
The swan flutters, the body withers.
Beating at crows, the arm grieves.
Says Kabir, the story sputters
and goes out here.

Once again a fish in the water.
In the last life I was drunk
on austerity. Heart detached,
I renounced family,
muttering only
Ram! Ram!
I renounced Banaras,
became a fool.
Lord, where am I now?
Was I a bad servant?
Were you unconscious?
Between the two of us, God,
who's to blame?
I came for your refuge
but couldn't find your feet.
I came to you!
Now the servant Kabir
is truly hopeless.

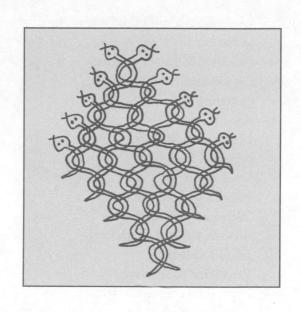

Is there any guru in the world wise enough
to understand the upside-down Veda?
Fire burns in water, blind eyes see.
Cow ate lion, deer ate cheetah,
crow pounced on falcon, quail conquered
    hawk,
mouse ate cat, dog ate jackal.
He who knows the primal teaching
is dressed right.
One frog ate five snakes.
Kabir shouts:
both together one!

This is the big fight, King Ram.
Let anyone settle it who can.
Is Brahma bigger or where he came from?
Is the Veda bigger or where it was born from?
Is the mind bigger or what it believes in?
Is Ram bigger or the knower of Ram?
Kabir turns round, it's hard to see—
is the holy place bigger, or the devotee?

What form or shape to describe?
What second one is there to see?
At first, no Om or Veda—
who can trace this ancestry?
No starry sky,
no moon or sun,
no father's seed,
no calm air,
sea or land—
who can name him
or know his command?
No night or day—

his race and family
who can say?

Remembering the empty, the easy,
a light broke out.
I offer myself to a being
based on nothing.

On that day neither air nor water.
On that day creation—who gave birth?
On that day neither womb nor root.
On that day neither knowledge nor Veda,
on that day neither sound nor sorrow,
on that day neither body nor house,
no earthly place, no sky or space.
On that day no teacher, no one to teach,
no difficult path, in or out of reach.

Of the sourceless state, what to say?
No town, nowhere to stay;
seen without a trace;
what do you call that place?

Say it: Ram's indestructible name.
If you leave Hari, there's no place to go.
Wherever you go, you're just a moth.
Do you see the trap? Then don't
burn. Get attached
to Ram's name, and learn
how the insect gives its heart
to the bee. The world is heavy
with the load of grief.
Creature, if you can think or see,
make an effort! Your thoughts are useless
waves, you can't see this shore
or the other.

The world: an ocean of desire.
Ram's support: a ship.
Take Hari's refuge: the sea will be
as wide as a calf's hoofprint.

No one knows the secret of the weaver
who spread his warp through the universe.
He dug two ditches, sky and earth,
made two spools, sun and moon,
filled his shuttle with a thousand threads,
and weaves till today: a difficult length!
Kabir says, they're joined by actions.
Good threads and bad,
that fellow weaves both.

First cleverness—not clever.
Second cleverness—who can know?
Third cleverness—eats cleverness.
Fourth cleverness—off they go.
Fifth cleverness—no one knows it.
Everyone is ruined in the sixth.
If you know the seventh cleverness, brother,
show it to me in the world
or the Veda.

The *bījak* tells of a treasure,
a treasure that doesn't show.
The word tells of a creature.
Only rare ones know.

The one whose name is unsayable, brother,
why sing a ramaini
to him?
The meaning—something like
a traveller on a boat, a
holding and letting go,
moving while sitting.
The body stays
but don't confuse
nature with dress.
Mind still.
Don't talk.

Mind goes without body,
body goes without mind.
Mind and body one:
Kabir says—there's a swan.

Culprit, you've missed
your human birth.
Many owners share this body.
Parents say, "Our son!"
and raise him for their profit.
Woman says, "My dear!"
and devours him like a tigress.
Fond wives and loving sons sit,
their mouths gaping like death.
Crows and vultures think
about death, dogs and hogs
eye the road.
Fire says, *I'll burn the body.*
Water says, *I'll quench the flames.*
Earth says, *I'll mingle with it.*
Air says, *I'll blow it away.*
You think that's your home, fool?
It's the enemy at your throat.

Dazed by swarms of sense-forms,
you call the flesh your own.

The body has so many sharers,
born and dying in pain.
Insane, entranced, unthinking man
shouts "Mine!" and "Mine!" again.

In front blazing fire,
in back lush green,
gives fruit when you cut the root—
homage to that tree.

Those who reached this town and didn't
get supplies got caught
in a storm, after dark,
where they couldn't
get supplies.

Swan, you're strong
but your habits are weak.
You're streaked with dirty colors
and screwing
with various lovers.

If I speak out I'm beaten.
When the veil's up, no one sees.
The dog hides under the haystack.
Why talk and make enemies?

Why is the doe thin
by the green
pool? One deer,
a hundred thousand
hunters. How to escape
the spear?

Half a couplet's on its head.
If it's set right,
then pandit, why bawl from the books
day and night?

Color is born of color.
I see all colors one.
What color is a living creature?
Solve it if you can.

Within the heart a mirror
but no face shows.
You'll see the face when the heart's
doubleness goes.

The road the pandits took,
crowds took.
Ram's pass is a high one.
Kabir keeps climbing.

Kabir's house is at the top
of a narrow, slippery track.
An ant's foot
won't fit.
So, villain,
why load your bullock?

Everyone says words, words.
That word is bodiless.
It won't come
on the tongue.
See it, test it, take it.

Take a vow, don't let go,
though tongue and beak are charred.
This is the way the moonbirds
chew hot coals.

Heart says: when to move?
Mind says: when to leave?
For six months you rack your brain.
The town is half a mile away.

A gown of love-silk—
put it on, Kabir,
and dance!
They shine with beauty
who speak truth
with mind and body.

Into the looking-glass cavern
the dog goes running.
Seeing his own reflection,
he dies barking.

The best of all true things
is a true heart.
Without truth no happiness,
though you try
a million tricks.

They don't listen to wise words
and won't think for themselves.
Kabir continues to scream.
The world goes by like a dream.

Drop falling in the ocean—
everyone knows.
Ocean absorbed in the drop—
a rare one knows.

Damp with separation, wood
smokes and hisses.
Sorrow ends only when
it burns to ashes.

Nearby they sink and don't come up;
it makes me wonder.
In illusion's swift stream,
how can you slumber?

You say the couplet but don't
grasp it. Your steps
don't make it.
The river rushes on:
where can a foot
be planted?

Many sayers, but no
graspers.
Let the sayers flow away
if they won't
grasp.

Clear things one at a time,
whatever can be cleared.
Whoever speaks with two mouths
gets slapped hard.

Good words, bad words,
back and forth goes the tongue.
Mind gives a hit:
this way and that.
It's Death behind the swing.

Point crammed into the body,
shaft broken.
Without the lodestone it won't come out;
a million other stones
have failed.

The worldling ponders:
domestic life or yoga?
He loses his chances
while others grow conscious.

It's the kind of speech
no eye can see.
Kabir says, listen
to the word spoken
in every body.

Grasp the root: something happens.
Don't be lost
in confusion.
Mind-ocean, mind-born waves—
don't let the tide
sweep you away.

The mind is a nervous thief,
the mind is a pure cheat.
The ruin of sages, men and gods,
the mind has a hundred thousand gates.

The snake of separation enters,
wounds the heart.
Sadhus don't flinch. If he likes it,
let him eat it.

Death is standing on your head.
Wake up, friend!
With your house in the middle of traffic,
how can you sleep so sound?

Wooden structure, black termite,
eating all he can.
Death dwells in the body.
No one understands.

Poor man! What to do?
He talks but the door won't open.
Put a dog on the ritual square,
he'll just lick up
the rice-powder there.

Poor man! What to do
with his empty body?
Not even a glimpse
of the creature appears.
At whom is Kabir shouting?

Try your best with jewels,
decorate the clay.
Kabir came and went again.
Existence is a lie.

Human birth is hard to attain,
you don't get a second chance.
Once a ripe fruit falls,
it won't jump back to the branch.

A raft of tied-together snakes
in the world-ocean.
Let go, and you'll drown.
Grasp, and they'll bite your arm.

If I say one, it isn't so.
If I say two, it's slander.
Kabir has thought about it.
As it is,
so it is.

Seeing a four-footed beast,
the hunter bolted.
What a marvel, seekers:
a corpse ate Death!

The three worlds were robbed,
everyone's everything taken.
The thief didn't have a head
so no one recognized him.

Seeing the mill turn
brings tears to the eyes.
No one who falls between the stones
comes out unbroken.

From monk you turned to thief,
from thief to social worker.
You'll never know what life is
till the blows come down on you.

Man in his stupid acts—
iron mail from head to toe.
Why bother to raise your bow?
No arrow can pierce that.

Parrot perched on a cottonwool tree
craves a couple of pods.
The pods go POP. The parrot
flies off in despair.

Don't display your diamond
in the vegetable stalls.
Tie it in the knot of the natural,
go your own way.

You don't find:
diamonds in storerooms,
sandal trees in rows,
lions in flocks,
holy men in herds.

All these people,
very proud of their own heads,
very far from Hari—
they'll never stumble
on knowledge.

How many days have passed
craving what's savorless?
Seeds don't sprout in barren ground
though torrents pour from the clouds.

Without living beings, beings can't live.
Life is the basis of life.
Be kind to beings, take care of them.
Pandit, think it over.

I don't touch ink or paper,
this hand never grasped a pen.
The greatness of four ages
Kabir tells with his mouth alone.

Moving within limits: man.
Moving without limits: saint.
Dropping both limits and no-limits—
unfathomable thought.

You have died and you will die,
the drums of death pound.
Like a dream-lover, the world fades.
One sign remains—a sound.

Who knows me,
I know him.
I don't care what the world
or the Vedas say.

He's bound by fetters,
the poor creature.
He can get free by his own strength
or the beloved can free him.

Don't murder a poor creature,
we all share one breath.
Though you hear a thousand Puranas
you won't get free of that death.

Three men went on pilgrimage,
jumpy minds and thieving hearts.
Not one sin was taken away;
they piled up nine tons more.

Oh virtuous vine,
none can tell your virtue.
From cutting the root you turn green,
from watering you wither.

Much thinner than water,
subtler than smoke,
swifter than wind,
Kabir's friend.

In an iron boat
loaded with stones,
a bundle of poison on his head,
he wants to cross over.

The mind, greedy for its own juice,
splashes in sensual waves.
Mind drives, body rides—
thus everything runs away.

The madman without a guru
blindly rushes around,
douses the fire on the garbage heap
and burns his own house down.

Do one thing completely, all is done;
try to do all, you lose the one.
To get your fill of flowers and fruit,
water the root.

In the wood where lions
don't tread
and birds don't fly,
Kabir ranges
in empty meditation.

Speech is priceless
if you speak with knowledge.
Weigh it in the heart's balance
before it comes from the mouth.

Use the strength of your own arm,
stop putting hope in others.
When the river flows through your own yard,
how can you die of thirst?

Into a lion's coat
rushes a goat.
You'll recognize him by his voice:
the word reveals.

A cage with ten doors,
a bird of air.
The wonder is that it's there;
no wonder if it goes.

Burning sand
in the body.
Everyone lives
in sorrow's shadow.

Where buyers swarm, I'm not;
where I am, there's no buyer.
Without awareness they wander,
plucking at shadows
of the word.

Jewels and stones fill the world;
a rare one tests them.
The tester is greater than the jewel—
so very rare!

A dreamer wakes from sleep,
opens his eyes and sees
the creatures are looting each other
and nothing is lost or gained.

I heard the instrument playing,
then all the strings snapped.
What can the poor instrument do?
The player's gone away.

You're a holy man? What are you
if you gab without thinking,
if you stab other beings
with the sword of your tongue?

A sweet word is a healing herb,
a bitter word is an arrow.
Entering by the door of the ear
it tears through the whole body.

See the diver's courage:
plunges in cold depths,
rushes past obstacles,
brings back the pearl.

This world is completely befooled,
they're missing both yoga and pleasure.
Kabir threshes sesame seeds,
the people thresh chaff.

If you're true, a curse can't reach you
and death can't eat you.
Walking from truth to truth,
what can destroy you?

Go home, doctor.
No one's asking you.
The one who put on this burden
will have to take care of it.

Teaching and preaching, their mouths
filled up with sand.
While they watched the fields of others,
their own crops were eaten.

I'm watching you,
you're watching him.
Kabir says, how to work it out—
I—he—you?

I'm looking at you, you're looking
somewhere else.
Damn the kind of mind
that's in two places at once.

Kabir recites couplets
every day right on time.
The dead do not come back,
no, they do not turn around.

What can the poor guru do
if the student's a lout?
Teach until you're blue,
you're blowing through bamboo.

No customers for the word:
the price is high.
Without paying you can't get it,
so move on by.

I didn't meet one heart's intimate:
all were full of their own needs.
Kabir says, the sky is ripped.
Can a tailor mend it?

I've seen them all burning,
each in his own fire.
I haven't met anyone
whom I could touch.

Makeshift man,
witless, weightless,
a red flower
without fragrance.

Straight-up trunk,
unreachable
fruit, a thirsty
bird that tried
hard. The fruit
is sweet, but so
far.

Glossary

BRAHMA   The Hindu creator-god, one of the three major deities (with Vishnu and Shiva) in the Hindu pantheon.

HARI   Epithet of Vishnu (q.v.), Kabir sometimes used by as a name for God.

KALIYUG   The last in the cycle of four ages, beginning with Satyug or the Age of Truth, and progressively degenerating until Kaliyug, when evil prevails and it is nearly impossible to know God or practice truth. At the end of Kaliyug comes an apocalyptic dissolution, after which the cycle begins again.

MAYA   Often translated as "illusion," *maya* actually refers to the phenomenal universe, the ephemera of transient forms. As these forms are always changing, going in and out of existence, they are "illusion." But Maya is also power—the power of finiteness, definition, bringing into form; and Maya is desire, for the existence of forms (including our own bodies) arouses a hunger to possess and control those forms. Sometimes Maya is presented as a concept; more often in Kabir it is personified as a powerful female being who leads people into craving and confusion.

PURANAS   General name given to collections of Hindu myths in Sanskrit; for example, the *Bhagavata Purana* contains the stories of Krishna's life on earth and the principles of Krishna *bhakti*. *Purana* means old.

RAM   The name of God most commonly used by Kabir. In popular Hinduism, Ram is the seventh avatar of Vishnu, King of Ayodhya and hero of the *Ramayana* epic. Kabir does not seem to believe in this anthropomorphic deity. Often he refers to "Ram" as a mantra, the Name, which is to be repeated over and over again by the devotee.

SHIVA   One of the three major Hindu deities (with Brahma and Vishnu), Shiva is the great yogi who practices austerities in the snows of Mount Kailash and is worshipped by members of the Nath sect and others who practice hatha yoga.

SHUDRA   Lowest of the four *varnas*, or major groupings of castes as defined in the ancient Hindu texts. Shudras are said to be born to serve the other three *varnas*, who are called "twice-born" and are much higher on the scale of ritual purity.

VISHNU   One of the three major Hindu deities (with Brahma and Shiva), Vishnu is the god who incarnates himself out of compassion for living beings, to save the world from overwhelming evil and to give his devotees a form to worship. Usually ten avatars are spoken of, though some scriptures list twenty-four. While Kabir does not believe in avatars, he often uses Vaishnava names for the supreme being (Ram, Hari, and in some collections Krishna).

YAMA   The Hindu god of death.

About the Illustrations

The illustrations accompanying these poems are traditional Indic ritual decorations, auspicious symbols, and floral designs, reproduced from Shanti Swarup's *The Arts and Crafts of India and Pakistan* (Bombay: D. B. Taraporevala Sons & Co. Private Ltd., 1956).

SHAMBHALA CENTAUR EDITIONS are named for a classical modern typeface designed by the eminent American typographer Bruce Rogers. Modeled on a fifteenth-century Roman type, Centaur was originally an exclusive titling font for the Metropolitan Museum of Art, New York. The first book in which it appeared was Maurice de Guérin's *The Centaur*, printed in 1915. Until recently, Centaur type was available only for handset books printed on letterpress. Its elegance and clarity make it the typeface of choice for Shambhala Centaur Editions, which include outstanding classics of the world's literary and spiritual traditions.

(Continued on next page)

FOUR HUTS
Asian Writings on the Simple Life
    Translated by Burton Watson

LOOK! THIS IS LOVE
Poems of Rumi
    Translated by Annemarie Schimmel

MIDNIGHT FLUTE
Chinese Poems of Love and Longing
    Translated by Sam Hamill

NARROW ROAD TO THE INTERIOR
    by Matsuo Basho
    Translated by Sam Hamill

ONLY COMPANION
Japanese Poems of Love and Longing
    Translated by Sam Hamill

PRAYER OF THE HEART
Writings from the Philokalia
    Compiled by St. Nicodemus of the Holy
    Mountain and St. Macarios of Corinth
    Translated by G. E. H. Palmer, Philip Sherrard,
    and Kallistos Ware

A STRANGER TO HEAVEN AND EARTH
Poems of Anna Akhmatova
Translated by Judith Hemschemeyer

THE TALE OF CUPID & PSYCHE
by Lucius Apuleius
Translated by Robert Graves

A TOUCH OF GRACE
Songs of Kabir
Translated by Linda Hess and Shukdev Singh